Terrain Training
for
Off-Road Runners

By

Stuart Fergı

TRAIL GUIDES
p u b l i c a t i o n s

First published in Great Britain in 2008 by Trailguides Limited.
Second edition published in Great Britain in 2011 by Trailguides Limited.
www.trailguides.co.uk

ISBN 978-1-905444-44-1

Trailguides Limited
35 Carmel Road South
Darlington
Co Durham DL3 8DQ

Cover design by Steve Gustard.

Contents

1. Introduction.

During the course of a run for a trail, fell or mountain runner you can come across a great variety of terrain. Loose rocky paths, peat hags, heather bashing and stream crossings are all common experiences during a trip for the true off-road runner. There are a number of factors such as territory, height, weather and landscape features which all ensure to make the outing not just a 'day out in the park'. To fully enjoy the excursion, it is important that you are prepared to cope with the challenge both physically and mentally.

Over the years there have been a number of studies which have praised the health benefits of outdoor activities with some research papers stating that "walking over uneven surfaces, as opposed to even surfaces (such as road or tarmac) reduces the blood pressure". It appears then that walking over bumpy ground while off-road activates a whole host of leg muscles that are not reached by level walking and they in turn help pump blood back to the heart. By implication then if this works for walking it surely crosses-over to off-road running compared to road running ?

In addition as part of the modern environmentally conscious world you should

Typical mountain countryside.

also be aware of the fauna and the environment around you as you run. Don't cause any damage by your passage through the country, be aware of the delicate balance of nature such as the delicate alpine flowers in the hillsides, leave only footprints as you run and not discarded rubbish. For most of us we are only visitors in the countryside, leave it as we would want to find it.

This book will help to prepare the runner who has limited experience of the off-road arena to understand what lies ahead when venturing further off the tracks and trails. The book will explore the different types of terrain you will encounter, the techniques for adapting your style of running to this environment, various safety aspects required to meet the challenge thrown up by the terrain and it will also look at some training patterns and methodology's that will help bring out the best of you while out on the "trail".

Glossary of Terms.
The following is a small summary of some of the terms used in this book.

Contouring – traversing across the side of a hill keeping to the same height.
Peat Hag - wet spongy ground of decomposing vegetation, with poor drainage, the soil is unfit for cultivation but can be cut and dried and used for fuel.
Scree – very small rocks on a hill side.
Sheep Trod – small track made by sheep.
Tussock – thick and tufty grass.

Typical trail running.

5

2. Physical aspects of running over ever changing terrain.

What happens when you run over a variety of terrain?

Off-road terrain is classified as all running surfaces other than road (tarmac) and athletics tracks. This encompasses a whole spectrum of surfaces ranging from dirt and gravel roads to field paths to mountain tracks. The surface itself can be solid and hard-packed or soft and boggy with all the different variations in-between. There may be obstacles on the ground such as loose stones or gravel, stiles or other objects both natural or man-made.

Running off-road has effects on both the runner's strength and endurance abilities (energy consumption) with both of these areas being examined in more detail in our other sister guides. In this guide we will concentrate on the effects of running on the terrain itself especially the aspect of the foot hitting the ground (foot plant) and how the normal running style has to be modified to efficiently move over different types of terrain.

Foot plant.

In an ideal running situation the foot lands on a hard level surface. The foot is then used to push the runner upwards and forwards in a straight line. However complications arise when running off-road as the foot makes contact with the ground at odd angles other than flat on the floor. This is caused by the unevenness of the ground or the composition of its surface, i.e. soft, boggy, stony etc, or a combination of these factors.

Running over such terrain means that each time you place your foot on the ground it may have a different feel, surface area and shape. This causes problems for the runner in two areas.
1.   Risk of injury.
2.   Ineffectiveness of running motion.

There are two main types of foot plant. Lateral (or sideways angle) and the front to rear plant.

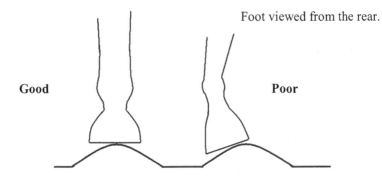

Foot viewed from the rear.

Good   Poor

Lateral plant – good.
The foot is placed level on the running surface with no sideways movement of the foot. Injury risk is minimal as there is no movement other than forwards and upwards. The effectiveness of the foot plant is high as there is no distraction and the push-off will move the runner forward and up.

Lateral Plant – poor.
The foot is not placed level and is rolling to one side of the running surface. Injury risk is high as the runner's weight when landing will encourage the sideways roll. The effectiveness of the push-off is reduced as the muscles in the foot and ankle have to counter the sideways movement while at the same time pushing forwards and upwards.

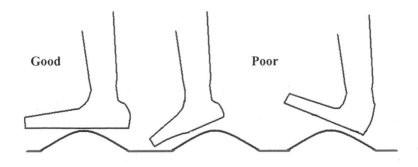

Good   Poor

Front to rear plant – good.
As with the lateral plant the foot is placed level on the running surface enabling the push-off to give upwards and forwards momentum.

Front to rear plant – poor.
Again the foot is not placed level but this time is rolling either backwards or forwards. As above the injury risk is higher and the effectiveness is lower.

Unfortunately (or fortunately depending on your point of view) running off-road presents a wealth of opportunities to experience the poor examples of foot plant. The rougher the ground surface then the higher the chances of meeting them. Some surfaces such as tussock and an undulating track could be a combination of both types of poor foot plant in the one movement.

The aim for the off-road runner when crossing rough terrain is to maximise the ideal foot plant as much as possible even if this means taking a slightly longer route. Being able to use the most effective running style as possible will maximise the overall running speed.

One exception to this rule is contouring or traversing around a hill, you do not use the ideal foot plant sequence but instead dig the outside of your shoe into the hillside. This is very stressful on the ankle especially if the hillside is steep. See Section 5.

Other running skills.

Many believe that there is no skill in running off-road. However being able to run effectively over terrain has a skill level as important as being able to run uphill and downhill and should be incorporated alongside the skills learnt in our sister guides that focus on these aspects.

There are four key fundamental skills to running across terrain namely:

1. Bounding – used for stream crossings and crossing features and/or obstacles.
2. High leg lifts – used when crossing heather, tussock, peat hags and other deep vegetation.
3. Fast feet – short, fast foot movements for steep loose rock and mud.
4. Balance – maintaining an upright position over all types of terrain.

We will explore some specific training aspects for these skills later in this guide in Section 4.

Conditioning the body to cope with the variety of terrain underfoot.

When conditioning the most important part of the body to concentrate on is the foot and ankle area. There is no substitute for running over off-road terrain to build up the strength and resilience in your ankles. However there are three sets of easy exercises that can be combined both with or without weights that will improve the strength of the lower limbs. The exercises are so straight forward that they can be done even while watching your favourite TV show.

The whole concept of these exercises is straight-forward enough. By subjecting the foot and ankle to a movement pattern that they are not familiar with then muscles that are used in the exercise are strengthened.

Exercise 1 – Left to Right.

Simply put, the exercise involves moving the foot from left to right.

Exercise 2 – Up and down.

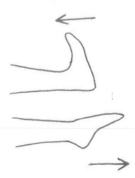

This involves moving the foot up and down.

Exercise 3 – Circles.

Point the toes out and then move them round in a circle.

Perform each exercise ten times then repeat with the other foot. Recovery will be the length of time taken to perform with the opposite foot.

One of the side-effects of these exercises is an increased mobility to the ankle area. Normally the ankle is limited in its range of movement purely because it is rarely asked to reach outside its comfort zone. Performing these exercises on a regular basis will push the movement pattern up to these limits and by repetition will then move and expand these limits outwards leading to greater flexibility.

Adding weights.

Ankle strengthening exercises can be improved by adding a weight, this can be as simple as filling a sock with sand or similar, tie a knot at the neck of the sock and then place between the big and the next toe and continue with the exercises.

See our sister guide on Strength and Conditioning for a more detailed look of how this can be achieved plus a more general look at the whole body.

3. Technical aspects of off-road terrain.

Types of terrain.

There can be many ways of representing the types or categories of terrain that you may encounter during your run, race or event. Each type of terrain may require a different style of running to run effectively across it such as shortening the stride length, increasing the stride length and braking or accelerating.

Terrain can be categorised as follows:

Track and trail.	Hard packed
	Loose rock
Steep hills and ridges.	Hard rock.
	Loose rock.
	Grass.
Off-track and trails.	Heather.
	Peat hags.
	Tussock
	Stream crossings
	Bogs and marshy ground.

These can then be further subdivided into:

Stable – when you plant your foot onto a stable section of terrain there will be no movement underfoot.

Unstable – when you plant your foot there will be movement which may unbalance you causing you to re-position during the foot plant in order to get back on course. This instability can be due to many factors for example the hard packed rock can have a crack, the grass may be wet, loose rock is inherently unstable except maybe when frozen, heather and other vegetation can be very hazardous as you often cannot see where you are planting your foot.

Rock.

Steep loose rock has many sub-terrains. The nature of rock underfoot depends on type and can have a very different feel. The stable/unstable barrier can be difficult to see. The main types are :

Hard Rock – granite where your foot sticks to the rock with no movement.

Fragile Rock – limestone where parts can break off causing foot movement.
Soft rock – sandstone , the surface area moves as the foot lands causing friction and further foot movement.

The most extreme end of this type of terrain is scree. Scree is a large area of deep, small rocks which when you run over it can be like marbles and can produce a small avalanche. In this type of running the technique is to lean slightly backwards digging the heals in and adjust to run with the rock movement underfoot. See Section 5.

Mud.
There a number of varieties of mud.

Surface mud. This is extremely slippery as the surface layer will move very fast. The mud will not be very deep and will act a bit like ball-bearings on the firmer surface underneath it.
Thick damp mud. This sticks to your shoes, adding weight to your feet and makes forward movement difficult due to your feet sticking to the ground like glue.
Deep spongy mud. Although the mud (peat)] does stick to your feet it is the spongy/bouncy nature of the foot plant that adds fatigue to your legs. Plus there is also the "shock" effect and risk of injury from suddenly sinking up to your knees.

Location effect.
It is clear that weather has a large effect on changing the conditions underfoot as does the location. In the low valleys especially on farm and agricultural land, mud tends to be thick and damp whereas higher up the slopes of the hill more surface mud is present and on the top of the hill you will find the deep spongy peat.

It is also evident that different areas give different grades of terrain. In the type of rock encountered, the English Lake District is predominately volcanic granite, whereas the Yorkshire Dales is limestone. However geology can always throw in a surprise and during the course of a short run in the mountains you can run over limestone, granite and then back to limestone. Let alone meeting sandstone.

Terrain – damage limitation.

All running presents risks from tripping, slipping and falling. However due to the nature of crossing uneven terrain, off-road running has a higher inherent risk and this risk can affect how you approach your training and your running style and speed.

When planning your run you may want to build in 'avoidance' by looking at your strengths and weaknesses compared to the different risk factors that may be encountered during the run. You may just be back from injury and may require a slow steady build-up over easier terrain to prevent re-occurrence. However no matter your level of fitness it is important to build strength to your ankles and legs to avoid risk and possible injury in order to fulfil a successful jaunt off-road.

Terrain	Trip	Slip	Fall Potential	Injury Risk
Tarmac	Low	Low	Low	Low
Track and Trail Hard Pack	Medium	Low	Low	Low
Steep Loose Rock	Medium	High	High	High
Steep Dry Rock	Medium	Medium	High	High
Steep Grass	Medium	High	High	Medium
Steam Crossing	High	High	High	Medium
Peat Hags	Medium	High	Medium	Medium
Heather and Tussock	High	Medium	Medium	High

Trip hazard – you catch the front end of your shoe on an edge and generally fall forward to the ground immediately in front of you.

Slip hazard – this is where the heel or side area of the shoe slips away from the terrain generally resulting in a fall backwards and landing adjacent to where you were running.

Fall potential – where you fall further away from your adjacent surroundings.

Injury risk – any injury suffered as a result of an "incident" will fall under a combination of three types.
Cut to the skin.
Break to a bone
Muscular twist or pull.

Route choice.

Planning.

Careful route choice at the planning stage can, in most cases, avoid the worst of the terrain or at the least present you with the least-worst scenario. Route choice is covered in more detail in our sister publication "Navigation for Off-Road Runners" however a brief overview of the effect of terrain and how it effects your decision is given below.

The fundamental question that you should be continually asking yourself is - is it GOOD or BAD terrain ahead. How much will I be able to run over this terrain or should I choose a different way.

It pays to know your map features and symbols and to be able to identify the least and most runnable terrain from a map. For example, the straight-line route below would go through the middle of a boggy area. Bogs or marshes are very unpleasant and nearly always impossible to run over especially if you end up waist deep in a peaty morass. Knowing the map symbols for marshy ground will help you identify this area before you even approach it and you could then plan a route around the bog which although may be longer in terms of distance will probably be quicker in terms of time.

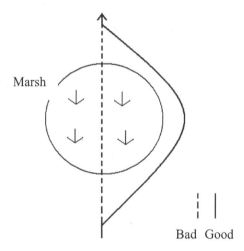

One trick that can be picked up from orienteers is the use of a traffic light system to help identify the nature of the ground that you are going to run over and the relevant amount of effort that you should be putting in. With virtually all off-road courses you will be unable to put maximum effort into the whole run, there are always going to be sections of the route where the terrain will be such as to slow you down. Effort should be saved for those sections where you will get the best return for it. Don't waste energy struggling to run through a bog when it can be better used on a long flat track.

At the planning stage it may help to identify those sections where you can run fast, those where you will need a slower pace and those where you may need to walk. The traffic light colours of green for fast, amber for slow and red for walk can then be assigned. It just helps you to remember and focus on a plan for your run.

Traffic light	What to do	Scenario	Pace
Red	Stop	Swollen stream Bog	Walk
Amber	Run with caution	Heather bashing	Slow to steady run
Green	Go for it	Sheep trod Forest track	Faster paced running

Unfortunately it is not always possible to judge the true nature of the terrain purely by looking at the map. This is where knowledge and experience of the area/route come to the fore. If possible always try to do a recce of the course beforehand, if that is not possible then you are going to have to take it as it comes.

However in either case always keep on the lookout around you, BE ALERT, for better route choices or worsening conditions underfoot. On the day you may always have to make short excursions en route if suitable opportunities arise, for example on a steep descent – it may be better to move off on a scree chute than descend on steep grass.

Picking a line.

Your speed over the ground is greatly reduced in difficult terrain and often there is a requirement to identify a route that will give the fastest running speed. This is known as taking a line. This does not necessarily mean following the straightest route as speed in off-road running does not necessarily mean going in a straight line but rather the shortest time from point A to point B.

Example of picking a line. Choosing a path between the tussocks of grass and the softer peat. Note also that by picking a different line the runner above has literally cut the corner of the route chosen by other runners as shown by the footmarks. This is a tactic that in a race can save valuable time and pick up places.

Always keep an eye open for 'Sheep Trods' especially when traversing grassy/tussock uphill areas – this will give you a chance to get in some much needed faster paced running. Often sheep trods are very narrow faint paths, here balance is very important and, as with downhill running, the arms are very important in order to keep stability.

Weather.

The weather can change the whole situation of the terrain you are running over almost immediately.

DRY   WET

When starting out it can be dry but rain can change the underfoot conditions dramatically. For example, you may have to change your running style as dry rock becomes wet and hazardous, you may have to slow down or even resort to walking and re-assess your run and may even have to change the route for a more comfortable and safe journey.

HOT   COLD

Again you can start off in good warm conditions but as you get higher and on an exposed ridge, a hail shower can provide an icy covering that can make dry rock into as slippery a surface as you can imagine. Again a re-assessment of the run may be in order.

The Four Seasons.
No not the band but Winter, Spring, Summer and Autumn. Although there very much seems to be ' well the winters are not as bad as when I was a youth' sentiment there is still very much a distinct change to the seasons unless you live on or near the equator. This change does not only affect your clothing choice but will also effect the condition of the terrain you will encounter while out for your run.

In summer you can have the effect of the heat drying out the paths and trails with the hard surface pounding your feet. Footwear choice may effect comfort rather than technicality. A thicker midsole may be the order of the day to provide cushioning.

In winter soft conditions may result in a more technical product being chosen for grip as the soft conditions negate the need for a thicker midsole. The soft conditions may change again due to frost and temperature change

Inclement Weather.
Weather can greatly change terrain, after torrential rain a dribble of a stream can turn into a torrent which can then be virtually impossible to get across, this then becomes a major safety hazard. You may have to look for an alternate route. A dump of snow can cover up underfoot obstacles never mind the slippage issue. A white-out in snow and dense fog can alter your perspective and may well require you to slow down, for collision or fall avoidance.

Rain.

In this country rain is the most common weather change but don't underestimate it as it is not just about donning waterproofs. Rain makes mud which can become a major slip hazard especially on slopes, it can also make grass as lethal as sheet ice. In wet conditions extra care needs to be taken on all upward and downward slopes.

Rain also has an effect on vegetation which in turn can impede your performance. When wet, vegetation such as heather, bracken and long grass becomes heavy and sticky and as you make your way through it, it can cling to your legs and slow down movement. At worst it can become a very real trip hazard.

In this country weather conditions can change quite suddenly with drastic results. Even on hard-packed trail a sudden downfall can produce a thin layer of surface mud which can be very slippery underfoot.

Running Style

Stride length.

The ability to alter your stride length quickly and even in mid-stride is a crucial factor in running off-track. Normally the endurance runner seeks to maximise their stride length. After all Stride Length x Leg Turnover = Speed, meaning that the more ground that is covered in each individual stride then the shorter the time to run over the ground.

So on the assumption above why would the runner need to shorten their stride length. The simple answer is to run safer and more effectively.

With a long stride length the first point of contact with the ground is the heel with the heel meeting the ground at an angle and the longer the stride then the more acute the angle. At the point of impact the bodyweight and power of the running stride is pushing downwards and if the contact surface is slippery this can cause the foot to move forward on contact thus causing a slip.

To prevent this the stride length will need to be shortened which in turn will normally mean that the foot plant will land with more of a flat sole. With a flatter sole there is less tendency for the bodyweight and power to generate forward movement on impact make the stride more effective and safer.

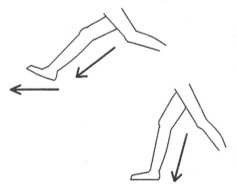

On a slippery surface the momentum on a heel strike can cause the foot to move forward on impact.

With a shorter stride and flatter foot plant the momentum does not cause the foot to slip forward.

Surfaces where the stride length would be altered include shallow/surface mud, snow and ice and even some not so obvious surfaces such as loose gravel or stone, wet leaves and grass.

Fast feet.

Fast feet is really a combination of quickly changing stride length, knee lift and the speed at which the runner's feet hit the ground and then take-off again. This is a technique that comes into it's own when running along a path that is rutted and obstacle strewn, for example.

Due to the nature of the path and the irregular spacing of the obstacles it is very difficult to maintain a constant running pattern. The placing of the feet has to be in a safe manner but also in a way that enables the runner to maintain his or her speed. Because the stride length is constantly fluctuating the speed of the leg turnover (the number of times that the foot hits the ground) has to be increased in order to maintain the same momentum. In effect, for example, instead of using four longer strides to cover an area of ground you would use eight to ten smaller petite steps but at a faster pace.

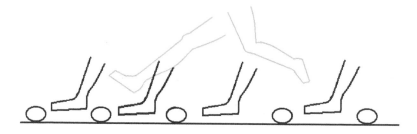

Instead of using a longer stride smaller steps would be used to place the feet in-between the obstacles but at a faster pace than that used with the longer stride.

Exercises for developing fast feet are discussed later in Section 4.

Leg lift.

Normally the endurance runner keeps the height of their leg lift to a minimum. Lifting the leg requires energy and this energy can be better used in ensuring that the runner travels further and faster and so the movement tends to just skim the feet above the ground.

This technique works when the running surface is level and flat however this is not always the case with off-road running. Terrain such as rocky paths, high vegetation and even stream crossings can all present trip and snagging hazards and can slow progress.

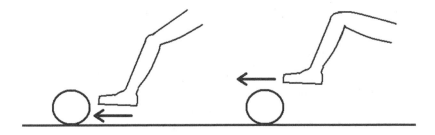

Obstacles on the path such as rocks, stones, branches etc can present a trip hazard and require the leg and foot to be raised higher to avoid them.

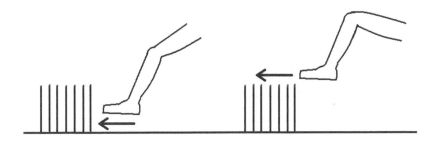

High vegetation such as heather and bracken or even long grass can snag the foot and leg as you pass through and become a high risk trip hazard. On top of that it can be very ineffectual as you try and force your way through the vegetation. The runner will effectively plough their way through the undergrowth. The more effective style to counter this is to adopt a higher knee lift to raise the feet and use a bounding style of movement to take you above the deep vegetation as opposed to going through it.

Many trails have an undulating surface and require the use of a higher knee lift to ensure clearance of the ground. In many cases the runner will be varying the height of the knee lift throughout the course of a run dependent upon circumstances and it will pay to develop the ability to vary the height at will.

Exercises to develop a higher leg lift are discussed later in Section 4.

Light foot plant.
As described previously, when the foot is planted it makes contact with the ground, normally with a heel first strike, it then rolls forward and the ball of the

foot and the toes push against the ground to drive the runner upwards and forwards. During the course of this action the runner's full bodyweight is supported on the one leg, this plus the effect of gravity means that every time that a foot is planted the runner lands with around three times their own bodyweight.

At times landing with this large impact can be a disadvantage such as

1.   When the ground is soft and the impact can cause the foot to sink making it harder to lift back out.

2.   When placing the foot on an obstacle such as a log or similar, in case the surface of the obstacle isn't solid or is slippery.

3.   When running through deep vegetation and the ground surface cannot be seen clearly. In this case there would be a reluctance to put the full body weight onto the foot in case it rolled resulting in some form of twist or sprain.

It is possible to run with what is called a "light foot" which means that you push-off with the foot before the full bodyweight has landed. This requires very good timing to start the push-off as soon as the foot makes contact with the ground. Some people are naturally more gifted at this technique than others, while some people just never seem to get the hang of it at all.

Unfortunately this is a technique that can't be used over long distances, it can only be used for one or two strides but during that time it can be quite effective at keeping you out of trouble. However at the same time it is one that does require practice to be able to control your movement and a good degree of strength in the muscles underneath the foot that power the push-off.

When practicing light foot plant start to think about the push-off movement before the foot lands and begin the movement of rolling the foot forward onto the ball of the foot literally a second before the foot makes contact. This is a difficult technique to master but can be done and when you have got it right you will instinctively know.

Balance.
As with all aspects of off-road running such as downhill and uphill running, a higher degree of balance is required to cope with the terrain than that required for a corresponding road run. The running surface is rarely level, the runner frequently has to cope with obstacles, the ground may be slippery, there may be a need to run on a narrow or thin path, there may be a steep drop to one or even both sides. There are many instances where the trail and fell runner requires a high degree of balance.

Never underestimate the effect of simply raising the arms out from the side. This technique is often used in downhill running but can also give advantages when used in the right context during more level running.

For exercises to develop your balance see Section 4.

Eye to Foot co-ordination.

Foot placement is key to both keeping your balance and successful forward momentum. Assessing the state and condition of the ground before you put your foot on it is essential to good foot placement. Use your eyes to look at the ground in front, try and plan where you are going to place your feet.

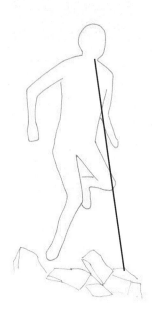

Focusing the eyes on the ground ahead helps you anticipate your responses to the ground. You may need to alter your stride length, slow the pace, use a light foot plant, jump an obstacle or even change direction. The sooner that you know that a potential difficulty is in front of you then the more time that you will have to respond.

Blind Feet.

This occurs when you plant your foot into long grass, heather or other vegetation and you cannot clearly see where your foot is landing. In these situations you have to expect some bad landings to result. Strong ankles that have been conditioned to take the knocks are the best insurance in these circumstances. Specific ankle strengthening exercises are described elsewhere in this book however one of the most effective methods of strengthening the ankles is by exposing them to the same experience as you will encounter in events. As the saying goes a little bit of what hurts them will do them good. A series of reps can be performed while running over this sort of ground. Practice by starting running in long grass in a flat field and progress up to tussock followed by heather and then to areas that you know have rocks hiding in the vegetation waiting to off-balance the runner.

Downhill rep through deep bracken. You can never be sure where and how the foot will land but by exposing the muscles and neuro-muscular connections to this experience during controlled training helps prepare them for the rigours of competition.

Mental attitude.

As with all running the importance of having the right mental attitude cannot be overstated. Knowing that you are fully able to meet the challenge of running over different and difficult terrain even in possibly adverse weather conditions only heightens the enjoyment of the off-road experience. It will also help enable you to run faster, longer and more importantly safer under all conditions.

To have a positive mental attitude requires pre-work and preparation and can be split into three factors.

Confidence.

Having the confidence in your own ability to complete your planned run is a valuable asset. Unfortunately this can only come from having done the hard work that builds you up to meet the challenge. There are no easy fixes for building confidence it comes from adequate preparation and proving to yourself that you can do it. Follow the steps below and you are almost there.

1. Prepare a correct training schedule that will train both your body and your technical abilities for what you are about to embark on.
2. Follow the schedule and do the training, if you don't its only you that will suffer.
3. Study the map and make sure that you are comfortable with the route, try and identify any areas that may cause potential problems and, if appropriate, plan an escape route(s) to use if conditions or circumstances change for the worse.
4. Go out and recce the route, run over it and see how it compares to the map and to what you expect, compare any areas that you have identified as possible problems to what actually lies on the ground.
5. If you can't get to the race route then at least do your best to train over similar terrain to ensure that you know what to expect.
6. Have a pre-race preparation plan to follow which will ensure adequate nutrition, fluid and rest.

If you have completed all these steps then you can be very confident about completing the run.

Focus.

Even with all the perfect pre-race preparation it is still quite possible to blow it on the day. Stay focussed on the event and what the day is about, pay attention to the detail and don't get distracted. Choose comfortable and appropriate clothing, do you have all the necessary and required equipment packed, do you have a map and is it the correct map, do you have adequate food and drink not only for the run but for the recovery phase afterwards. Simple points but ones where many runners in the past have fallen over. Even at the event stay focussed, follow your normal warm-up routine and get yourself ready for the start.

Concentration.
The key to running over difficult terrain is concentration. This shows itself in watching where you put your feet, looking ahead to determine the correct running line, keeping an eye open for potential hazards and just generally being aware of what is going on around you. Being distracted and losing concentration can and does result in accidents happening. These may be minor such as just taking the wrong line and adding seconds onto your time or it could result in something much more serious such as a fall and possible injury. Try and keep the running and the distractions separate. If you want to be distracted by, for example, looking at the view then stop, take a breather and enjoy the view. Don't try and do it at the same time as running .... !

Footwear.

Road running shoes are not suitable to run off road. Terrain trashes shoes, sharp rocks can lacerate outsoles and heather can test the durability of upper materials.

When choosing your footwear for the run, look at the terrain very carefully. Some fundamental questions maybe but ask yourself is the majority of the route on....

Terrain	Yes	No
Muddy, peat hags with no paths.		
Hard pack trail.		
Loose rocky paths.		
Rye grass, heather with no paths.		

Is the weather forecast.....

Weather Conditions	Yes	No
Wet		
Dry		
Cold		
Hot		

Is the route generally.....

Elevation	Yes	No
Steep		
Flat		

These type of questions will help you decide the footwear choice, see pages 30 and 31.

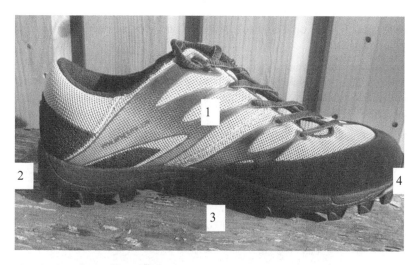

Anatomy of an off-road shoe.
Fell shoe above, trail shoe below.
1.   The upper - for comfort and stability.
2.   The midsole - for cushioning.
3.   The outsole - for grip.
4.   The rand - for protection (optional, not on all shoes - for example on the fell shoe above but not on the trail shoe below).

Here we will focus on the outsole, off-road running shoes which come in two generic varieties :

Trail shoes – these generally have a variety of short rubber sole patterns and have, generally, a thicker midsole offering which provides more cushioning. Fell shoes – these have large rubber studs on the outsole and a very low profile design.

So the choice between the two for a particular run takes into account a number of factors, mainly.
1.   terrain.
2.   weather conditions.
3.   elevation .

Outsole of two typical examples of fell (top) and trail (bottom) shoes showing the marked difference in sole pattern which gives the different degrees of grip between the two types of shoe. Note also the slimmer profile of the fell shoe which aids in contouring across the slopes of hills and also increases stability when on rough terrain.

So taking into account our damage limitation from the questions at the front of this section.

If you are on a hard pack trail, dry conditions or the route has little or no climbing then a trail type shoe may be more suitable than a fell shoe, as the greater volume of rubber on the ground will grip better..

If you are on a route mainly across peat hags or wet conditions with some steep climbing then the fell shoe may be more suitable due to the additional grip of the long studs.

Top Tip.   Right grip for the right terrain is of the essence.

Looking after your shoes.
After each run it is always best to wash your shoes, this not only gets rid of mud and foreign object to the inner and outer or outsoles but clears out any dangerous chemicals that you may have run through. Take out the footbed, the removable insole of the shoe, when drying.

Typical mountain tracks, here at Chamonix.

Accessories.

Metal Studs
Many orienteering shoes have metal implants set into the rubber studs on the sole. These give a firmer stud and can give extra grip during snow and icy conditions and especially when running over rock. If using these be aware of the environmental damage that will be caused by the studs "scratching" the surface of the rock.

Gaiters.
Foreign objects such as stones, pieces of vegetation and even grains of sand in the shoe can cause discomfort and lead to blistering which can have the potential to quite literally stop your run. Nowadays there are a number of gaiters on the market specifically for runners, as with the walker's gaiter they are designed to reduce and even stop debris getting into your shoe. If running some of the more extreme events such as the Marathon Des Sables, see photo below, then gaiters become more essential, in this case to stop the sand entering the shoe. Gaiters come in four types.
1. attached to the shoe.
2. gaiter which fits around and over the shoe.
3. attached to the sock.
4. custom or home made.

Waterproof Socks.
There are a number of these products on the market which can work remarkable well especially with shoes that have an open mesh upper. In this case the open mesh will move the water away from the shoe's inner allowing the waterproof sock material to work. These socks are quite effective and can give dry feet over a variety of weather conditions although as a downside the socks themselves do tend to be heavier than more normally constructed socks. The only real problem with the waterproof sock is when you enter water that is too deep and the water then runs over the top of the cuff around the ankle and enters the sock. This can cause discomfort as the sock is unable to wick away so much water and can result in the feet getting cold and the run becoming uncomfortable. In most cases a normal high wicking sock is the usual best compromise for all conditions.

Running bottoms.
Thermal tights, tracksters or running bottoms are generally used in colder weather to keep the legs warm. However they are also very useful as protection for the legs by helping to prevent abrasions, scratches and small cuts when running through deep and prickly vegetation or closely planted woods.

Gloves.
As with tights, gloves not only can be used as hand warmers but also for hand protection from abrasions, scratches and cuts especially when running over rocky and hard terrains where there is a requirement for a high degree of hand contact with the surface and also the potential for a high fall or trip risk.

Safety considerations.

We have looked in depth at slippage and trip hazards plus the effects that weather can have on the terrain. We will now explore some other items of safety that you should be aware of. General safety issues such as clothing, weather, etc are covered in the sister book "An Introduction to Trail and Fell Running". Here we will look at items that are more terrain specific.

Midges.

This insect can be a real pain especially if you are allergic to their bite. Not all areas of the country suffer from them. To give a very general idea of the distribution of this spring, summer and autumn problem see the chart below.

UK AREA	MIDGE RATING
Scotland	*****
Lake district	***
Kielder, Northumberland	*****
London	0 ?
N Wales	***
Peak District	***
Yorkshire Dales	**
Dartmoor	*

Midges do not like the cold and normally die off with the first cold snaps of autumn. However when in season forests, rivers and areas of damp vegetation are prime locations that seem to attract the little beasts.
There are a number of ways to deter the midge.
1. wear a midge net over your face and cover up the rest of your body.
2. spray on deodorant or insect repellent.
3. electronic devices.
4. joss sticks, not practical while running but works at overnight camps.

If you do get bitten carry some creams which sooth the area to keep inflammation and irritation at bay. Seek medical help if required.

Ticks (Lyme Disease).

Ticks seem to becoming more of an issue in certain parts of the country. As you pass through dense undergrowth, ticks can jump and attach themselves to your body. Although not usually infectious, some can carry Lyme Disease which does have the potential to be serious and in rare cases fatal. Removing ticks from your body can be a problem as the front end of the tick, the head, burrows into your skin to feed on your blood. It is important to get the whole body out including the head. Leaving the head in can cause infection.

Some of the more traditional methods of removal are no longer accepted practice, for example:
1.   Do not leave the tick in until they drop off.
2.   Do not attempt to pull out with tweezers as the probability is that you will leave the head inside.
3.   Do not cover the tick with petroleum jelly or alcohol as in some cases this can make the tick sick and cause it to vomit into the blood stream.
4.   Do not use the hot head of a burnt match or cigarette end as it rarely removes the head.

Instead special tick removal tools can be obtained from most vets or pet shops. Although designed for animals they are usually just as effective on humans.

Seek medical help if at all worried about the effects of Lyme disease.

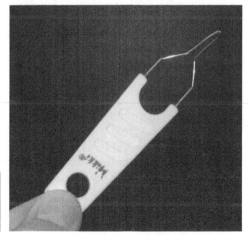

A specialist tick hook which makes removing the tick a very easy operation

Snakes.

Generally snakes are no problem as they will hear you coming and move out of the way but on occasion especially on warm sunny days they will bask on open paths or tracks and often fall asleep. Beware as you may tread on one or more likely, just as you are about to place your foot on it, it wakes up and starts to hiss at you. This can be pretty unnerving and can give a sudden shock however in these cases the snake is normally just issuing warning to back-off and an actual bite is rare. Just avoid the snake and run round it.

In the unlikely instance of being bitten, adder venom, although potentially lethal, is not particularly strong or fast-acting. Nowadays death from a snake bite in this country is extremely rare however it is still vital that you attend a hospital as soon as possible.

Moorland Nesting Birds.

Some species of birds such as curlews and grouse nest in the undergrowth of the moorland floor. This is particularly common in open access countryside. Some races are seasonal due to restrictions imposed during nesting, to protect the birds, their eggs and young. Try to re-arrange your route to avoid nesting sites and if you come across a very verbal and dive bombing bird then retrace your steps back and re-route to reduce the stress on the bird and possible damage of eggs and the young.

Even outside the breeding season one particularly annoying aspect of moorland birds is their insistence on remaining still until you are virtually on top of them and only then do they take to the air. Strong nerves and the ability to withstand sudden shocks are sometimes needed on a run across the moors.

Obstacles.

During the course of running off-road you will encounter many obstacles which again must be traversed with care. Tree roots, boulders, rocky ridges, steep sided gorges, walls and fences, gates are prime examples. You may need to use your hands to get over the obstacle or maybe just a good foot plant and a leap will be sufficient. Quite often you will need to alter your running style.

Stiles.

One obstacle that is worth discussing in more detail is the stile. You will come across stiles while running off-road anywhere in the country and they come in many shapes and sizes including some very tall and steep ladder stiles. Stiles are either wood or stone and occasionally are quite elaborate. They are high-risk when wet or damp and also when fatigued towards the end of a race. Stiles can often cause bottlenecks in races which as a result can cause you to feel hurried when crossing the stile. This pressure can increase the risk factor resulting in slips and trips. Take extra care under these circumstances.

However no matter the situation use the stile and do not be tempted to climb the wall or fence. Any damage caused by such activity can be a severe headache for the race organiser and in some cases has resulted in the landowner threatening to withdraw permission for the event.

Temporary Ground Covering.

What lurks under that pile of leaves, gravel, snow, ice pool of water ..... you may find out the hard way with a fall or slip that could result in injury. Be observant and if necessary slow the pace down and modify your running style.

Steps.

Many paths and trails now have erosion control paving complete with stone steps and flags. These can be very slippery and a trip hazard especially when wet.

Even when dry, steps and flags will interrupt your stride pattern and your running style which itself can have a knock-on effect on safety. Often you may come across wooden boards which are again very slippery and always watch out for the broken board and the beckoning hole.

Both stone and wooden step paths can be found on some steep terrain. These erosion control methods are there for a reason so use them rather than the adjoining areas. Do not add to the erosion problems.

Steep Terrain.

While climbing (or descending) up through gullies or on a hillside always be aware of loosening or dislodging any rock that may fall behind you onto those behind. This is particularly relevant in scree or with loose rock on steep hillsides. Out of courtesy to other hill users use the recognised mountaineering shout of "below" if you dislodge or see any falling rocks or boulders.

Stability.

When running downhill it is essential to use the arms for stability and balance to help prevent falling, see our Sister publication 'Downhill Techniques for Off-Road Runners'. Using arms is also important when running over rough terrain for example:
1.   Balance for narrow tracks and ridges.
2.   Strength to assist bounding through deep heather.
3.   Assisting balance by touching the ground when moving up or down steep terrain.

Exposure.

In this context we are talking about steep drops not weather associated exposure. On ridges and steep ascents you will come across exposed areas. Some people

or one of your party may have a fear of heights, if you have the choice then choose your route carefully to avoid such areas. If not slow down and take things easy. Be careful to avoid any slips and trips and if possible try to stay away from the exposed edge of the path as much as possible.

Load Carrying.

When running with a rucksack or bum bag your running pattern will be altered due to the weight of the sack and that will also change your centre of gravity and how your body responds to the different patterns of terrain. There is no substitute to practising running with your sack or bag and conditioning your body to the different stability and movement patterns.

4. Training techniques for terrain running.

Simple single exercises
These can be used as part of a warm-up routine, part of a complex training session or even as a single rep session in its own right. There are four areas to look at which correspond to the four fundamental skills shown on page 8.

1. Bounding and jumping
When running off-road there is often a need to negotiate obstacles and even crossing streams can be a common occurrence. Bounding is a common exercise throughout this series of books and the benefits and principals of it are explained elsewhere in the series. However here we will look at two specific exercises, one to build strength and the other as a means of measuring your strength and ability.

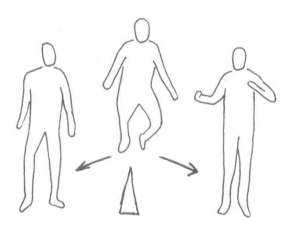

Jumping from side to side with feet together.
From a standing start with the feet together jump sideways. Recover and then repeat back to your original position. An obstacle such as a cone or small hurdle can be used to jump over and provide a target for height gain.

This exercise helps improve elastic strength which provides the explosive force when leaving the ground be it as part of a jump, leap or your normal running stride. The movement sideways helps improve mobility especially when moving in a different angle to the normal straight ahead.

Bounding is simply an exaggerated running action. Push-off with the left foot and bring the leg forward with the knee bent and the thigh parallel to the ground. At the same time, reach forward with the right arm. As the left leg comes through, extend the right leg back and it is kept extended for the duration of the push-off. Hold the extended stride for a brief time before landing on the left foot. Repeat with the right leg.

Use lines on the ground to give an estimate of the distance covered in each particular bound. An alternative would be to count the number of bounds needed to cover a set distance i.e. the width of a football pitch. The fewer the number of bounds needed then the greater the distance covered in each bound due to the higher strength level.

2. Forward and upward movement – leg lifts.
Running through deep vegetation such as heather requires a greater degree of upward movement than normal running over a good surface. This requires an element of bounding plus the ability to perform a high leg lift when required. This may also involve some side-ways movement.

The body is a marvellous thing but does tend to learn movement patterns by rote, that is by repeatedly doing them. Once ingrained it can be fairly difficult to adopt a new pattern and over the years most runners have only become accustomed to lifting the knees as high as is required for the running stride. This can give problems when this requirement changes and the knees need to be lifted higher than the norm.

The following exercise is designed to exaggerate the knee lift and as such accustom the runner to raising the legs that bit higher.

Perform as either a walking or slow running exercise although initially it may be better performed as a walking exercise until a degree of competence has been

reached. Walk or run and as you do so raise the knees as high as you possibly can. This will also involve an overly exaggerated arm movement as well. Perform this over thirty metres, have a walk back recovery and then repeat.

As competence increases it will become possible to use small hurdles to help enforce the knee lift.

3. Fast feet

Pitter-patters
This is an exercise performed while slowly jogging and is designed to stimulate quick leg movements emphasising ankle extension and flexion. The exercise should be performed over a short distance typically 30 metres but maybe shorter if performing the exercise for the first time.

The runner moves slowly but moves the legs and feet quickly to obtain as many

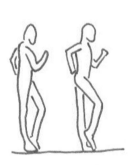

foot strikes as possible in the distance. Stride length should be short and as soon as the foot hits the ground it should be lifted again. Treat the ground as if it were a red-hot surface and you would obviously want to keep your feet on it for as short a time as possible. This exercise is called pitter-patters because the runner effectively pitter-patters across the ground.

An alternative to pitter-patters is an exercise often used in other sports. It follows the same movement style as pitter-patters but uses a laid-out grid to help determine the stride length. This is very similar to running along a series of tyres as has often been seen in the Hollywood sporting films.

The grid is comprised of narrow squares following on each other very much like a ladder with its rungs. Because the squares are narrow the stride length is restricted and the idea is to run along the grid placing a foot in each square as quickly as possible therefore stimulating foot speed. Grids on string can be purchased from specialist sporting goods stores or can be just laid out with chalk or flour. As opposed to squares, circles can be laid out alongside each other which makes it look even more like a line of old tyres.

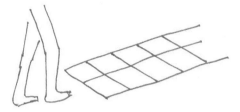

For those that can remember such a thing try a game of hop-scotch. Again as above the trick is the speed movement. I'm not sure how well introducing a game of hop-scotch into a training night will work but be experimental and give it a go.

4. Balance

Balance is a notable feature of all terrain running. Good balance is essential to off-road running. Balance can be improved by using such artificial aids such as wobble boards and even tight-rope walking. Not as daft as it sounds as you can use the tops of walls and fences or even a piece of timber laid along the ground.

Balance 1 –Wobble board device or tight rope, wall or fence top.

A number of artificial aids can be used to help develop balance, the most well-known being the wobble board which is the bottom half of a sphere beneath a flat board with the obvious intention of maintaining your balance while standing on it. Another balance exercise among some climbers is using a tight rope, which they call slack lining or walking along the top of a wall or fence . An alternative for those who don't fancy the cost of the wobble board or the height and safety element of tight rope walking is to just place a long narrow length of wood such as an old-fashioned clothes prop along the ground and walk along it as if it were a tight rope. Sounds silly but it is effective.

Performing drills can give the impression that you have gone slightly daft. However don't be put off by the embarrassment factor, they are effective and do work and you will get the benefit from all this fun.

Balance 2 – Toes on edge of kerb or step, lift up and down. Fairly easy exercise to perform and one that doesn't need any equipment other than a kerb or step which are normally readily available. As the description says use the toes to balance on the edge of the kerb and then slowly lift yourself up and down on the toes. You will find that in order to keep your balance there will be a need to outstretch the arms.

This exercise also has the beneficial side-effect of strengthening both the feet and ankle muscles.

Balance 3 – Stand on one leg, lift the other leg off the ground and hold for ten seconds. Repeat for the other leg.

The easiest exercise of all to perform with no equipment at all required. Initially you may need to outstretch the arms to maintain balance but as you become more proficient the need will diminish and also the time for which you can continue the exercise will increase. The exercise can be made more difficult by slightly bending the supporting leg at the knee to keep you more off-balance.

As with the toe exercise above this also has the beneficial side-effect of strengthening both the feet and ankle muscles.

Constructing an individual session for terrain training.

One of the golden rules of training and one that is taught to most coaches at the start of their careers is that of specificity, making the training specific to the event. This also applies to off-road running and especially to terrain training. As we have already seen off-road running encompasses a wealth of different types of conditions and terrain.

If you are training for a specific competition then your training needs to reflect the conditions and terrain that you would expect to meet in the actual race. It is not adequate preparation to perform all your training in a dry mountainous area with a good path system if the event is being held over pathless boggy upland moor and vice versa.

Individual training sessions can be designed to improve any aspect of off-road running including the ability to cope with rough and difficult terrain. Many runners tend to train at what they enjoy and what they enjoy is, surprisingly, what they are good at. Be prepared to examine your running and determine what you are not very good at, namely your weaknesses, nine times out of ten this will be an area that you don't enjoy but be prepared to tackle this head-on and both ability and enjoyment will follow

As an example, a weakness has been highlighted as 'running down steep loose rock'. A range of sessions have been constructed to help rectify this with a progression in three stages.

Stage 1.
A 30m long easy angle, loose rock slope. 10 Reps.
Rep 1-2 Slow pace.
Rep 3-5 Increase speed.
Rep 5-7 Max comfortable speed.
Rep 7-9 Reduce speed.
Rep 9-10 Slow pace.

Stage 2.
A 60m long medium angle, loose rock slope. 12 Reps.
Rep 1-2 Slow pace.
Rep 3-5 Increase speed.
Rep 5-8 Max comfortable speed.
Rep 8-10 Reduce speed.
Rep 10-12 Slow.

Stage 3.
A 100m long steep angle, loose rock slope. 12 Reps.
Rep 1-2 Slow pace.
Rep 3-5 Increase speed.
Rep 5-8 Max comfortable speed.
Rep 8-10 Reduce speed.
Rep 10-12 Slow pace.

As both you and your body become familiar with running this type of terrain you will become more relaxed and the maximum comfortable running speed will increase.

Move in between the stages when you feel comfortable and safe to move up.

This basic model can be used for constructing any of the following sessions :

running across heather or tussock.

running across peat hags.

running across or up and down on loose rock.

running up or down on steep grass.

running up or down steep rock.

running across hard pack trail or track.

The parameters laid out above are not hard and fast and terrain sessions can be made very flexible. The basic concept is that specific terrain training will improve your ability to run over that type of terrain. After that it is down to your own imagination to come up with sessions that will rectify short-comings in your ability and then implementing them.

To construct your rep you may want to utilise the area next to a good track for the rep. The track can then be used for the recovery leg to avoid any undue stress on the feet and ankles. See the picture above showing a session over heather.

Putting it together into a more complex session.

It is possible to combine the individual reps and build them into a more complex session that can make the best use out of any area that is available to you. However be aware that if you want to focus on specific weaknesses then it may be necessary to travel to a different area that has the desired terrain.

For example a 10 km run is sectioned in 5 x 2 km parts.

Distance in Km.	Stages	Terrain	Technical aspects
1 to 2	Warm Up	Hard Pack Trail	Include some bounding and leg lifts as part of the warm-up.
3 to 4	Technical	Stream Bed	Wet rock and steep loose rock.
5 to 6	Strength	Heather	High knee lifts and bounding.
7 to 8	Technical	Forest	Obstacles and fast feet.
9 to 10	Taper	Hard Pack Trail	Finish with mild stretching.

A visual illustration of the session is shown below.

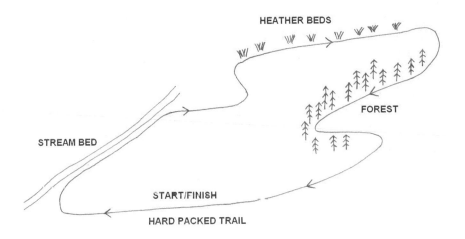

How often should you do a terrain specific session

For a normal time-constrained runner there is always going to be a compromise between what you would like to do and what can actually be fitted into a busy week.

Continuing the theme of a four week macrocycle that was started in the sister books "Downhill Techniques" and "Uphill Techniques" a specific terrain training session can be built into the training program every fourth week. Bear in mind that if constructed properly the downhill, uphill, fartlek and up and down sessions will also include an element of terrain training even though their primary purpose would be conditioning for hill work.

It would also be assumed that the weekend long run would be over appropriate off-road terrain. Here again even though the primary purpose of the session would be long-distance endurance the secondary effect would be terrain conditioning.

	Week 1	Week 2	Week 3	Week 4
Tuesday Quality Session 1 Hill session	Downhill Reps	Uphill Reps	Structured fartlek or an up and down session	Terrain training
Thursday Quality Session 2 Speed session	Speed	Speed	Speed	Speed
Saturday	Undulating threshold run	Undulating threshold run	Undulating threshold run	Undulating threshold run
Sunday Weekend Run	Long run including rolling hills	Long run including rolling hills	Long run including rolling hills	Long run including rolling hills

	Primary Effect	**Secondary Effect**
Downhill Reps	Hill work	Terrain conditioning
Uphill Reps	Hill work	Terrain conditioning
Fartlek	Hill work	Terrain conditioning
Terrain	Terrain conditioning	Hill work
Long Run	Endurance capacity	Terrain conditioning

Always remember that if you are aiming your performance towards a specific event then the terrain training element should be geared towards conditioning the body for the terrain that you will encounter.

Stretching.

As with all aspects of running, stretching is a very important part of tapering/ warming down after a terrain session. However this should be gentle stretching as opposed to a hard physical pull to the muscle. Four examples of the most important stretches after a terrain session are:

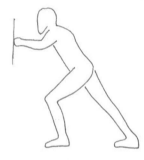

Calf
Stand arm's length away from a wall. Keeping the rear leg straight, bend the knee to lean into the wall. The stretch will be felt in the calf of the rear leg. Hold for 30 seconds and then repeat with the other leg.

Hamstrings
Sit with the legs outstretched. Without bending the knees slowly bend forward from the waist until the hands touch the toes. Hold for 30 seconds feeling the stretch down the back of the leg.

Quadriceps (thighs)
Stand on one leg. With one hand grasped around the ankle bring the non-supporting leg back until the heel touches the buttocks. Hold for 30 seconds. Feel the stretch in the front of the thigh. Repeat with the other leg.

Ankles
Kneel on something soft such as an exercise mat. Remaining kneeling, slowly lift the right knee off the ground leaving the foot in contact. Feel the stretch along the front of the ankles and the lower shin. Hold for 30 seconds and then repeat with the other leg.

Remember that stretching after a hard session is part of a recovery phase and should always be MILD stretching and never taken to extremes. Hard training sessions can cause micro-tears in the muscle fibres which can then be aggravated by violent stretching. And in all cases never prolong stretches to the point of pain.

5. Practical examples.

The classic endurance running style is concerned with running as fast as possible while using the least amount of energy. This gives a running movement with the arms close to the side and moving backwards and forwards, slightly crossing the body. At the same time the body is held vertical with a slight lean forwards. Stride length is not too long and the thigh is not lifted as high as in fast-paced running with the foot skimming just above the running surface.

When running off-road this classic style still holds true as being the most energy efficient method of running. However in every off-road run there are sections where this optimum style has to be modified to cope with the specific requirements of particular terrain. In these circumstances the most economical manner of running is not the most practical or the most efficient.

In the following pages we will look at a number of specific terrains which will require adjustments to the normal running style.

Training notes.

Assumption that the session is to be performed over the appropriate terrain.

Repartition (rep) : a single run performed over a short distance at a faster than normal running pace.
Set : a group of repartitions.
5k pace : the speed that you would normally run a 5k or 3 mile race at.
10k pace : the speed that you would normally run a 10k or 6 mile race at.
Walk/jog back recovery : slow paced recovery in-between repartitions taken as a walk or slow jog back to the starting point.

Scree Running.

Key skill: Balance

When entering a scree area, you will quickly notice that the earth moves beneath your feet due to the loose nature of the small stones over which you are running. Do not panic into making a notable change of stance instead lean your body slightly backwards and push your heals back into the slope as you descend and move in time with the movement of the small rocks beneath your feet. Don't be tempted to race or slow down, just relax and go with the movement of the stone. Imagine that you are snowboarding down perfect deep champagne powder snow in Colorado. Scree running is fun, but be aware that the rocks also move down the slope therefore ensure that there is no danger to anyone below you. The safe descent of a scree slope can be a challenge for you and anyone in the surrounding area.

Training.
The critical element for running down scree is balance. If it is known that there is going to be an element of scree running during a race route then regular exercises to refine and improve balance need to be incorporated into the warm-up or as a specific session.

Heather Bashing.

The UK does have some pretty deep heather fields on
the top of its moors. If the need is to traverse a heather field at a fast pace then it
becomes necessary to use a high knee lift to raise the feet and bound across the
deep fauna. Keep your body upright and use the leg lift technique combined
with using your arms in a synchronised motion to help lift the whole body.
Momentum must be maintained, if you slow down you will end up walking
resulting in ploughing through the heather rather than bounding over it.
Bounding is less tiring that ploughing.

Training.
Referring back to the construction of an individual session on Page 45, once the
ability to run through heather has been developed the standard session to
improve would involve a series of repartitions of between 100 and 200 metres
through a heather bed. The session would be between 3 and 5 sets of 12
repartitions with a 10 minute recovery between sets and a walk/job back
recovery between repartitions.

Ridge Running.

Occasionally you get the need to run over sharp edges
and ridges such as Striding Edge in the Lake District. Ridge running requires
concentration and good balance with accurate foot plants. It is unlikely that you
would be able to run but being able to move fast and safely along such features
is one of the most satisfying aspects of mountain running. Confidence in your
own ability is essential for such terrain along with having the necessary skills.
Both of these can be built-up slowly and steadily by walking the route and also
by working your way up through the scrambling grades. If necessary consider
hiring a qualified mountain guide to help learn confidence and build up these
skills.

Training.
The critical factor for ridge running is balance. If it is known that there is going
to be an element of ridge running during a race route then regular exercises to
refine and improve balance need to be incorporated into the warm-up or as a
specific session.

Stream Crossing.

Key skills: Bounding and balance.

Crossing a stream can be divided into two options.

1. Keeping dry - whenever possible use a bridge or if unable, then try jumping over the stream, entering the water automatically increases the risk factor. Jumping will involve utilizing your bounding skills.

2. Getting wet - walk through the water. Crossing a stream is inevitable in some events and you are going to get your feet wet sometime. Choose your crossing point carefully, look for shallow areas without fast flowing water. Keep your balance by using your arms and moving slowly. If the water is deeper or if you are not running alone then put your team working skills into place and hold hands to increase balance, four legs are better than two sometimes. However if alone, walk across the stream at right angles to the water flow, this will reduce the pressure from the stream flow.

Training.
Be familiar as possible with stream crossings and where possible deliberately build them into your long run.

Contouring.

When traversing at the same height around a hill side and are running across an angled slope you are putting great stress on the ankles and lower limbs. You cannot expect to go out in the hills and complete long stretches of contouring without conditioning and strengthening your lower body. There are five areas to assist in competent and injury free contouring.

1. Dig the outside of the running shoe into the hillside to help prevent slipping down the slope of the hill, see the diagram below.
2. Angle the body and lean into the hillside for balance.
3. Keep one foot exactly in front of the other, see Narrow Paths and Sheep Trods for the technique of doing this.
4. Where possible look for sheep trods to follow, the running will be slightly easier.
5. Shoe selection – choose a fell shoe with studs to be able to cut into the hillside, a trail running shoe has too thick a midsole for safe contouring.

With running across the slope of the hillside it is always worthwhile bearing in mind the effects that weather can have on the ability to contour. Wet weather be it rain or just low cloud can make grass very slippery making it very difficult to

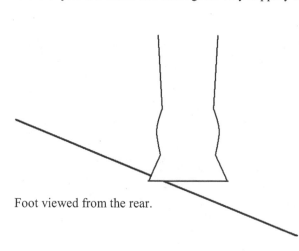

Foot viewed from the rear.

run across the slope. Snow and ice can have the same effects as can frozen earth. Steeper slopes that you can run across in fine weather can turn into no-go areas when the weather turns inclement. The wind can present problems especially when contouring across the open exposed hillsides making balance a real effort to "get it right".

Digging the edge of the outsole into the surface of the slope helps to prevent slipping down the slope.

56

Training.

Contouring normally involves running for a longish distance round the side of a hill so any training sessions should reflect this endurance aspect and should be taken at a slower pace but over a longer distance.

Typical sessions would involve repartitions of between 800 and 1,000 metres taken at 10k pace. Dependent upon ability and nature of the event training for, the number of reps would be between 5 and 10 with a recovery between each rep of half the time that it takes to complete the repartition. The recovery would be taken at the end of the rep and the following rep would return to the starting point.

When running across the slope of a hill angle the body and lean slightly into the hill.

Snow

Snow obviously occurs during the winter months although it is possible to get a flurry "out of season". The other major factors to govern the possibility of snow are location and height, the probability and effect of snow is greater higher up in more mountainous regions than it is on a lowland park run. However during the winter months it is always beneficial to watch the weather forecast, this will help you to plan ahead and anticipate such things as:

1. To determine if snow has already fallen above a specific height so that you can plan your run and equipment beforehand.
2. To determine the likelihood of snow falling during your run.

Snow itself presents a number of hazards:

1. It presents a major slip hazard particularly when the ground slopes even if the slope is only a minor one.
2. It covers the ground and obscures obstacles giving both trip and fall hazards.
3. In severe conditions such as a white-out it can present visibility problems which, as an understatement, can give severe health and safety problems.

Whereas we tend to think of snow as just snow it can be very different in nature. Three examples are:

Powder. Deep snow of champagne-like texture which generally means more and higher leg lifts as you run through it. For long downhill's a running style similar to scree running should be used. The deeper the powder the more demanding on the legs and the more physically exhausting the run will be. This and the increased time that would be taken should be factored in when planning longer runs in a landscape where you would expect snow.

Ice. Possibly the main reason why runners take a tumble during winter. Ice can be a major hazard especially when covered by snow and unseen. Observation and recognising spots where ice may form can help prevent an accident. Watch out for signs, for example does the area look like it was boggy, are there any rivers nearby, does it look as if water has run-off across the path, is there a hole in the ground that may contain ice.

Slush. Normally found lower down in the valleys and during a thaw. This can sometimes be a slip hard but more importantly as a risk factor it will get you wet, really wet around both the feet and the legs and once wet your limbs very quickly become extremely cold.

Changing temperature both over time and as a result of changing altitude, has a vital role in snow as the condition of the snow and associated weather can change quickly. Always be prepared to amend the route and duration of your run if conditions deteriorate. Safety first.

Be prepared for the weather, not only with the correct clothing and health and safety equipment but also with the choice of footwear as it can become critical. When running in snow preferably wear studded shoes possibly with metal implants, at the least wear very deep-soled shoes.

Care must be taken with foot placement. Shorten the stride length to avoid landing on the heel and try to keep the body weight over the foot as it lands on the ground as opposed to a normal stride where the body weight is at an angle to the foot and will push the foot forwards causing a slip.

In deep snow there may be a requirement to use a high knee lift.

Training.
As snow is highly weather dependent specific training sessions based on the repartitions format is not particularly practical or guaranteed to happen. However as a crucial factor of running over snow covered terrain is the ability to perform "fast feet" then during the back-end of the year more emphasise should be placed on including a fast feet drill into your warm-up procedures.

Surface mud

Can occur anywhere particularly during
or after rain in which case you tend to have a thin layer of mud which can move
over the top of the harder sub-base.

Surface mud presents a major slip hazard particularly when the ground slopes
even if the slope is only a minor one.

Care must be taken with foot placement. Shorten the stride length to avoid
landing on the heel and try to keep the body weight over the foot as it lands on
the ground as opposed to a normal stride where the body weight is at an angle to
the foot and will push the foot forwards causing a slip. If necessary be prepared
to outstretch the arms to aid balance.

Training.
As for snow however because surface mud can occur at any time during the year
you should have a regular inclusion of a fast foot drill in the warm-up.

Deep mud

Deep mud can occur anywhere but is normally along a man-made track or path where movement either by vehicle, man or animal has churned up the surface. Deep mud on open ground such as the high moors has been classified as "Boggy Ground".

Dependent upon the time of year, the weather and the volume of use of the track, the length and depth of mud on these sections will vary. One particular area that gives problems is around gates where the congregation of livestock can create very deep mud coupled with copious volumes of dung.

Avoid if possible as ploughing through the mud is lung and leg bursting running. Pace will be slowed quite often to a walk but sometimes momentum can be maintained by effectively jumping from firmer piece to firmer piece although this may involve weaving from side to side and travelling a longer distance than the straight line route.

Not only is running in deep mud hard work but also very messy. Like glue, mud will stick to both your shoes and legs giving extra weight to carry. At times this

build-up on the shoe sole may need to be scraped off by scuffing the feet as you run.

There is a high slip factor as the studs or tread on your shoes will probably not penetrate deep enough into the mud to make contact with firm ground. This can be compounded by mud building up under and around the sole making the studs/tread totally ineffective. At times this can seem as if you are wearing a pair of glass-bottomed platform boots.

In more open areas such as around gates, deep mud can totally dry out during the heat of summer. This can result in a very hard rutted surface which can be treacherous to run over and will normally mean a reduction in speed and extra care to avoid turning of the ankle.

Training.
Deep mud, boggy ground and sand are very strength and endurance sapping and the basic parameters of training are similar.

Because of the strength/endurance element required training sessions for this terrain should be taken over a longer distance typically 800 to 1,600 metres and taken at between 5k and 10k pace. The number of repartitions would be between 5 and 10, the longer the distance the smaller the number of reps. Recovery between reps would be between half the time it takes to complete the rep and equal to the time that it takes to complete the rep. Recovery would be at the end of the repartition with the next rep returning to the start.

Boggy ground

Key skill: Short stride length.

Normally encountered during fell runs over high ground. Peat bogs can be quite deep and can stop all running resulting in the need to resort to walking (or wading in some cases) to make your way through them. Some boggy areas may be quite narrow, forming just a border either side of a small stream, in which case it may be possible to leap across. Where there is a choice try and avoid these areas, unfortunately this may not be an option if a race route has to be strictly followed.

Bogs can present a hazard as suddenly sinking to any great depth can give a shock to the system and has the potential to strain muscles.

Boggy ground can normally be identified by the rushes and the bright green sphagnum moss that grows in the vicinity. By being observant and reacting quickly enough the worst of the bogs can be avoided.

There are no magic techniques to enable you to run through a bog, ultimately if the bog is sufficiently deep and large you will end up walking. However bear the following in mind :
1.   Be observant and watch the runners in front and if they sink in a soft,

Growth of rushes indicating boggy ground.

deep spot then avoid that spot.

2. If the mud is not too deep then a previous runner's footsteps may have compressed the mud to a level where it will not sink any further, in which case run in their footsteps.

3. People tend to avoid the deep spots which can create a number of paths round the outside of these spots. This can be confusing as in the jumble there may be no clear line to follow. In these situations try and identify your exit point before you enter these areas.

Training.
See Deep Mud although the training surface would change to boggy ground.

Boggy areas may be extensive but the individual bogs themselves may be sporadic and there may be runnable terrain between the areas of soft ground. Here observation is the key in being able to identify where you can run and where you need to walk.

Narrow paths and sheep trods

A sheep trod is a thin narrow path created by repeated use by sheep. They can often be found contouring round the side of a hill and can be a joy to run on. Quite often these are a great deal more effective to follow than bashing your way through the heather however be aware that sheep do meander and while a trod may start heading out in the right direction to follow there is no guarantee that it will stay heading that way so be aware of your direction and don't blindly follow.

Both narrow paths and sheep trods may be walled in on either side by deep heather and/or tussocky grass. This means that escape from the path may be difficult or may mean literally jumping out of the path.

There is a very distinctive running style needed for these narrow paths. The normal position of the runner's pelvis mean's that the legs hang down with the feet beside each other and when you walk or run this is continued with your left foot to one side of the right. With narrow paths this "wide" foot plant may be too wide for the actual path with the result that the runner actually puts their feet in the vegetation on either side of the path.

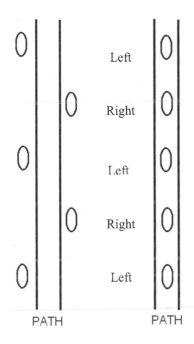

A modified running style needs to be adopted where the runner actually places their feet in more of a straight line, one in front of the other. This ensures a good foot strike and a safer forward momentum. The diagram to the left illustrates both styles.

Running one foot in front of the other obviously has an effect on the balance and can create a slight "wobble" with the result that although most runners can do it many of them do have a reduced running speed. Regular practice can familiarise you with this technique and help ensure a higher speed when traversing narrow paths.

Normal running style.

Modified running style.

Practical examples of moving along a narrow path. Note that the feet are placed in a straight line one in front of the other rather than alongside each other during the normal running gait as shown on the head-on photo on the next page.

Training.

Training for this type of running is more skill based and can therefore be performed over shorter distances. Once the ability has been established using the exercises on Page 45 then the normal session for this type of training would tend to be 100 to 200 metres. Speed would vary as the crucial factor is to develop the skill and balance. The session would be of 3 to 5 sets of 10 repartitions with a walk/jog back recovery between reps and a 5 minute recovery between sets.

Hard-packed trail

Hard packed trail is generally man-made either for vehicle or pedestrian use. The surface may be hard packed as part of a deliberate construction such as a vehicle track or just through years of repeated use, for example, a walker's path. Be aware, however, that some walker's paths in the more scenic parts of the country are deliberate constructions.

Because of their varying types of use, hard packed trails come in different widths from being capable of providing access for sixteen-wheel articulated timber wagons to the width of a single walker but generally they can be classified into two types.

Smooth and hard-packed such as the forest road shown on the next page. In these cases there is no need to modify the running style and you can just concentrate on maintaining a high running speed for as long as possible working on the assumption that some of the following sections of terrain may force a later slow down in pace.

67

Rough and littered with objects such as stones and tree roots for example the mountain path shown on the previous page. This presents a high trip risk which means that you have to concentrate on foot placement. This will involve focussing your eyes on the ground several paces in front of you and possibly slowing down and altering your stride length. You may also have to use the fast foot technique with short fast movements of the legs and feet and occasionally the arms to aid balance.

Sections of erosion or over-use may turn the surface of a smooth hard packed track into a rougher one particularly on a slope where a water course is liable to flow over the track. Despite the temptation to run on auto-pilot stay focussed on the track ahead and if or when necessary change the running style.

Training.
Normally prepared for during sessions for other aspects such as speedwork and tempo runs.

Virtually all off-road runs and events will contain a section of hard packed trail of some shape or format during the course of its route. In particular the section leading to and from the start/finish line is normally deliberately chosen as a wide track in order to avoid congestion when the race starts. Worth bearing in mind if you are thinking of a sprint finish.

Rough pasture

Rough pasture with grass tussocks
can occur in most areas of the country from open moor to semi-cultivated
grazing land. This presents a real problem for the runner as the surface of the
ground is never really level due to the tussocks plus there is always the
insecurity of placing the foot down only to have the surface collapse underneath
your weight.

Make no mistake this is ankle busting running and for any runner new to
off-road running this is a vital area to develop. The main emphasis for running
on this terrain is having strong ankles and as a priority this should be worked on
either by familiarisation and regularly running over tussocks during training,
individual strength exercises or even better, a combination of both.

Try and focus the eyes ahead and identify good foot placements. This may
involve putting the foot in-between individual tussocks of grass and using the
feet-in-line technique from Narrow Paths. Quite often it will involve placing the
foot actually on the tussock but always be aware that the surface underfoot may
be weak tufts of grass that can collapse and jerk your foot to one side with the
result of real stress in the ankle area and in worse case, injury. In these situations
if you are quick enough, it may be possible to use the light foot technique and
avoid planting the full bodyweight thus helping you to recover before you go
fully over on your ankle.

Be prepared to use outstretched arms to aid your balance especially in the event of a bad foot plant which could lead to a stumble or fall.

Fast running across rough pasture is high risk basically because high speed means less time to respond to possible problems with foot placement plus the momentum from faster running will be more likely to cause a fall in the event of an ankle twist. Where necessary reduce speed on these sections.

Even for properly conditioned runners long stretches of running across this type of terrain can really fatigue the ankle muscles making them sore for a long period after a run. A lengthy period of more gentle running may be necessary to aid recovery.

Training.
The aim of any session here is to develop ankle strength and balance without making the session too long that the ankles become too sore to continue.

Typical sessions would be between 200 and 400 metres in length with 10 to 20 reps depending on distance chosen. The total distance of the reps being 4,000 metres. Reps to be taken at 5k pace with a walk/jog back recovery.

Tussock grass often occurs on the sides of hills where the land is not cultivated and is just left for grazing. This can add to the problems of running up or downhill.

Loose stone

Key skill: Erratic stride lengths.

This can be found at any angle, uphill downhill and on the flat. You really have to concentrate – foot placement is key but also you have to be aware of ground movement during the foot placement cycle and be ready to use your upper body to re-align yourself for the following placements. A fall can be a serious injury risk especially on the downhill aspect.

Care needs to be taken when running over loose stone as the stone may present both a trip and a slip hazard. If necessary slow the speed down and focus the eyes ahead to identify any possible trip hazards. Try and ensure that the stones on which you place your foot have a solid grounding and will not move as you place your weight on it.

Be aware that even small stones such as gravel can be a slip hazard when travelling at speed particularly on sloping ground due to the angle at which the heel strikes the ground. Be prepared to alter your stride length to give a flatter foot strike if necessary.

Training.
See Rough Pasture although the training surface would change to loose stone.

Loose stone is not just a feature of mountain tops but can also be found along stream and river beds.

Sand

Not normally considered but it is surprising how many events there are around the coast of the country and beyond that do include at least one section on sand be it from the beaches of the Northumberland Coastal Run to the more exotic foreign climes of the desert and the Marathon de Sables.

Sand is a very exhausting and strength sapping medium to run over and can be split into two types, soft, loose sand and hard-packed. As you'll imagine, on coastal runs hard-packed sand is normally caused by the effect of the tide although in sheltered areas it can, as in desert regions, be caused by other factors. Hard-packed sand is always going to be the preferred choice to run over and whenever possible look for trails which will be more solid even if this means running close to the waterline. This will speed up the running and avoid the leg exhausting deep and moving sand.

Foot placement is not generally an issue in these locations as there is not usually many foreign objects to worry about although on soft sand there may be slight movement of the foot on impact.

When running down sand hills or dunes adopt a similar style as scree running, shown earlier in this section. Although smaller than scree, the grains of sand will have a similar movement pattern and will move down the slope with you.

One thing to note is that sand really does get into your shoes which may sound flippant but does have the potential to give serious problems. Grains of sand in the shoe can become an irritant and lead to blistering of the feet. If an event contains long stretches of sand running then it may be worthwhile considering some form of gaiter to prevent the sand getting in.

On the plus side, if you do fall over on sand then at least on most occasions it will be a nice, soft landing !!

Training.
See Deep Mud although the training surface would change to sand.

Gnarly bits

Key skill: All of them.

Every now and again you come across a
piece of terrain that doesn't fit into the normal description due to the number of
obstacles and trip and slip hazards. For want of a better name I've called these
"gnarly bits". In the example shown below, you can see a woodland path
heading downhill where the path is criss-crossed by exposed tree routes and to
make things even worse, the path is literally covered with stones of various
shapes and sizes with some of the stones being loose and some embedded into
the earth. This sort of terrain doesn't just occur in woods and can just as easily
occur on more open land and even moorland with heather roots combined with
stones.

This presents almost every type of trip and slip hazard and is very difficult to
run over especially for those new to off-road running or the less experienced.
The risk factor here is obviously very high, even more so in wet conditions
when both roots and rock can become very slippery.

The key to keeping a momentum going over this type of terrain is foot
placement although in truth virtually every skill that is covered in this book

74

would get used over this terrain.

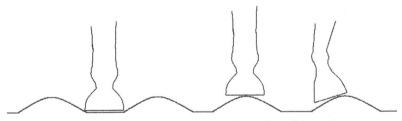

Foot viewed from the rear.

Foot placement.
As far as possible try and place the foot on solid ground in-between the various obstacles this will help reduce any slip/trip risks and will also ensure a smooth push-off from the ground. In many cases you will find that it is almost impossible to place the foot in this position and you will have to place it on top of the obstacle itself. In this case always try and put the foot on something that is solid and firm. Anything that is likely to collapse or roll away and thus cause injury will do so, always err on the side of caution. When placing the foot down on one of these obstacles remember what was said about foot placement in Section 2 and always put the foot on the top of the stone, root or whatever the object is. Placing the foot on the side may cause the foot to slip and/or the obstacle to roll.

Stride length.
The stride length will be constantly changing as you look for a secure foot plant. Most of the strides will be short in length but you will often find that no two strides will be the same length.

Balance.
Essential due to the slipping and tripping hazards. Use outstretched arms to help and if necessary stop and re-balance yourself before commencing again. Better this than trying to run while off-balance then losing it and having a fall.

Fast feet.
Because of the short stride lengths necessary you will find that you will have to move the feet faster in order to keep momentum going. However as with the balance if at any point you feel that you are moving too fast for safe control then

be prepared to stop and re-align yourself.

Eye to foot coordination.
Essential to view the ground ahead as you run in order to decide where you put your feet. Keep the eyes focussed at least two or three steps ahead of yourself.

Confidence.
Moving fast over this sort of surface requires a high degree of confidence in your own ability and faith in where you are placing your feet. When first confronted by this type of gnarly ground it can be very off-putting and intimidating. Regular practise will help build confidence as well as your ability.

Training.
This is the sort of terrain where walk-through reps can both help ability and confidence. Quite simply walk through a stretch of fifty to one hundred metres of suitable ground. As you become more familiar with the necessary techniques and movements increase the pace to fast walking and then to slow jogging. Eventually this will develop into a slow run. This terrain will never lend itself to a sprint but at some point you will arrive at a speed at which you will feel comfortable with and at which you can control your reactions.

6. Summary.

To be able to run more confidently and smoothly, and knowing what hazards to expect as you run through a diverse range of terrain will only help the enjoyment of the off-road runner. Being able to understand the aspects that various types of terrain has on your running style and being able condition the body both physically and mentally can only help towards a safe traverse of our varied countryside.

Our terrain and environment is precious – so look to protect by running sensibly and taking heed to all environmental codes of conduct.

On your next run off road you will now look at your environment with a different perspective.

The author exploring the local trails around his home in the Durham Dales.

About the Author

Stuart Ferguson is a member of the Fell Runners Association, a founder member of the Durham Fell Runners club and a UK Athletics coach specialising in Endurance Running in the Fells and Mountains.

Stu has been an active outdoors person for over thirty three years indulging his passions as a fell runner, rock climber, mountain biker and skier in areas as far apart as the USA and Nepal. He currently lives in the Durham Dales.

Stu has been an active long and ultra distance runner for many years competing in numerous events around the country under the trail, fell and LDWA banners. In 1998 and 2001 he was the winner of the Durham Dales Challenge 28 mile off-road run. He has also advised on and supported a number of challenge attempts by fellow runners notably on the 72 mile Bob Graham Round in the English Lakes.

Looking for new challenges he has devised and ran in 2005 the inaugural Durham Dales Reservoir Round of sixty miles in under twelve hours and in 2006 the Durham Hewitt's round of forty eight miles in fourteen hours. Current plans include a seventy two mile round of all the current Youth Hostels in the North Pennine area.

A summary of his other accomplishments include:

- His mountain marathon record includes:
  Open Country MM 2002, 4th overall, 1st vet team.
  Lowe Alpine MM 2004, Elite 9th overall, 1st Vet team.
  Lowe Alpine MM 2005, Elite, 12th overall, 1st Vet team.
- First duathlon style round of the 4 x 3,000 feet Lakes peaks in 11 hours 34 minutes including running Scafell and Scafell Pike and mountain biking Skiddaw and Helvelyn.
- First mountain bike round of the High Street and Helvellyn Ridges, 54 miles in 10 hours 15 minutes.
- A rock climber with 84 x 1ST ascents from Cornwall to Northumberland including Spitfire E3 5c Aire Rock, Cornwall; Sacked E1 5b White Tower, Pembroke; Marquee Metal E3 5c Wanney's Northumberland and First Born, Direct Finish E5 6b Kyloe, Northumberland.
- Walked the Pennine Way, West Highland Way and the Helumba Trail in Nepal.

Has skied over twenty winter seasons, the majority in the French Alps with many classic off-piste descents including Valle Blanche in Chamonix.

Currently Stuart coaches fell and hill running through his club, Durham Fell Runners and the Run Off-Road organisation as well as managing his own outdoor consultancy and equipment testing company   **stuffmountain**

Acknowledgements

This coaching book has been a real challenge, exploring new ground (excuse the pun) and at times wondering how to get to the end result. Without the encouragement and support of many people, this project may well have never been finished.

To the people below, thanks, it would have been a lot harder without you.
Gillian Ferguson
Sam Ferguson
Emma Ferguson
Tim Barnes
Patrick Bonnett
Will Horsley
Roger Kleppan
Steve Lumb
Mike Mallon
Tim Makin
Harry Manuel
Keven Shevels
Mike Tyrie

To all members of DFR, my group and individual clients that I have coached, thank you for letting me experiment !

The Run Off-Road Series

Run Off-Road is the name adopted by Trailguides for it's publications aimed at the fell, hill, trail and mountain runner. This series of books is designed to promote the sport of off-road running in all it's many forms and to encourage the participants to improve and develop their abilities and skills in order to further increase their enjoyment of the sport.

This is an evolving series of books that is constantly expanding. See our website at www.trailguides.co.uk and subscribe to our newsletter for regular updates on our range of publications.

At the time of writing the titles in the series include:

An Introduction to Trail and Fell Running
Downhill Techniques for Off-Road Runners
Uphill Techniques for Off-road Runners
Terrain Training for Off-road Runners
Mountain Marathon Preparation
Navigation for Off-Road Runners
Long and Ultra Distance Off-Road Running

Coming soon
The Mountain Marathon Book

Disclaimer

The information contained in these pages is provided in good faith, but no warranty is made for its accuracy. The contents are, at the time of writing and to the best of my knowledge, up-to-date and correct. However, the world is a changing environment and what is correct one day may not be so the next. The suggested training regimes contained in this publication are exactly that, suggested. It is the reader's responsibility to judge their own level of fitness and whether they are capable of performing any of the said activities.

No guarantee whatsoever is provided by the author and his team and no liability is accepted for any loss, damage or injury of any kind resulting from the use of these pages. Nor as a result of any defect or inaccuracy in them.

As with all outdoor activities, you and you alone are responsible for your safety and well being.